TAKING PART

Community Helpers

by Sally Hewitt

Photographs by Chris Fairclough

This edition 2006

Franklin Watts
338 Euston Road
London NW1 3BH

Franklin Watts Australia
Hachette Children's Books
Level 17/207 Kent Street
Sydney NSW 2000

ISBN-10: 0 7496 6662 5
ISBN-13: 978 0 7496 6662 0
Dewey Decimal Classification: 371.19
A CIP catalogue reference for this book is available from the
British Library.

Printed in Malaysia

Editor: Kate Banham
Designer: Joelle Wheelwright
Art Direction: Peter Scoulding
Photography: Chris Fairclough

Acknowledgements
The publishers would like to thank the staff and pupils of
Branscombe Church of England Primary School, Devon, for their
help in the production of this book. We would also like to thank the
National Trust for permission to reproduce their logo. Photographs
on pages 7, 16, 20b, 21, 23t, 24, 26 and 27 were kindly supplied
by Branscombe School. The photograph on page 8b was kindly
supplied by the Alliance and Leicester Building Society.

Contents

(Words printed in **bold italics** are explained in the glossary.)

Your *community* is all the people who live in the same *neighbourhood* as you, so you are a member of your community. The children of Branscombe Primary School are members of the community of Branscombe.

↑ This is Branscombe village.

Branscombe School has only 60 pupils.

Welcome to Branscombe

Branscombe is a seaside village surrounded by farmland. It has a church, two pubs, a Post Office and a village hall. Lots of people come to Branscombe for holidays, so there are also guest houses and camping sites.

Community projects

Every year, the children and teachers of Branscombe Primary School plan a major community project. They know it will be hard work, but people from the local community give whatever help they can. One of the teachers explains, 'We are fortunate that so many people share their talents with us.'

Previous projects

The Remembrance Garden in the churchyard and the **Millennium** Orchard both started as school community projects. The school has also produced a useful Parish Map (below), written and illustrated by the children and their parents.

> *You help out in the village and be part of our community.*

The children explain what it means to be a good citizen of Branscombe.

> *You help raise money for the village.*

People can sit peacefully in the Remembrance Garden. ↓

BRANSCOMBE PTFA PARISH M

Any money raised from sales of the map goes towards equipment for the school. ↑

The Community Fund

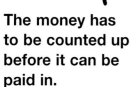 This year's project is to set up and manage the Branscombe School Community Fund. The children organise special *fund-raising* events, and the money raised is put into a *building society* account.

The children enjoy visiting the building society to pay in their money. ↑

The money has to be counted up before it can be paid in.

The Alliance and Leicester

A member of the Alliance and Leicester Building Society came to the school, and told the children how *interest* on the money in their account will help it to grow. Now the children know that the more money they raise, the bigger the fund will be and the more the interest it will earn!

Whom shall we help?

If anyone, adult or child, feels that help is needed anywhere in the world, a school meeting is called and they agree whether to send money, and how much. They may decide to send £100 to a **disaster appeal**, or buy a bunch of flowers for someone in the village.

If we see something on the news and want to send some money there, we know we've got money in the bank.

The children explain why the Community Fund is a good idea.

It's a good idea because the money keeps on adding up.

The children split into groups to come up with lots of money-raising ideas. ↑

Question

Which of the fund-raising events listed here do you think would raise the most money?

choosing the events

The children discussed money-raising ideas, then voted for the ones they thought would be the most fun and would raise the most money. These are the ones they chose.

- Non-uniform week
- Bring-and-buy sale
- Plants, cakes and pickles sale
- **Sponsored** spell
- Lucky dip

Mad Hair and Scary Wear

Everyone wants to be involved in choosing the themes.

The first fund-raising event was non-uniform week. The children had to choose a different theme for each day of the week.

> We go into groups and come up with ideas, and the whole class chooses which ones they like best.

These are the themes they chose for non-uniform week:

Monday
book character day

Tuesday
mad hair day

Wednesday
scary wear day

Thursday
red, white and blue day

Friday
impersonations day

50p please!

Anyone who wanted to come to school in non-uniform had to give 50p to the community fund. Some children dressed up every day. That cost them £2.50! They gave their pocket money or asked their families and friends to make a contribution.

All kinds of characters turned up on Monday.

'We're having a good time and raising money too.'

A red, white and blue flag was hung outside the school on Thursday.

On Wednesday, the safest place to be was at home!

Stories came to life on Friday.

Question

Why do you think non-uniform week was such a success?

A brilliant start
Non-uniform week was a great success. £141.00 was raised to start the fund off.

For the bring-and-buy sale, the children brought in old books, toys and games to sell. Even though they didn't want them any more, someone else might.

↑ Before the sale started, the children wrote a label for each item saying what the price was.

The soft toys were very popular. ↑

Running the stalls

They set up the stalls and decided how much to charge for all the items. If something cost too much, no one would buy it; if it cost too little then money was lost for the community fund.

Attracting customers

There was no excuse for anyone to miss the sale. The children made posters and sent out a newsletter with all the details, so that everyone could come and join in the fun.

Bargains

If anything wasn't selling very well, the stall holders reduced the prices. There were some good bargains!

> *You have to be responsible to run a stall, because you have to look after all the money.*

Number crunching

A great deal of maths is involved in running a stall. You have to decide how much to charge for each item. If someone buys several things, it's important to be able to add up quickly and to give the right change.

The last job of the day was to count up how much money was raised.

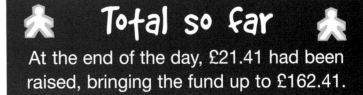

Total so far

At the end of the day, £21.41 had been raised, bringing the fund up to £162.41.

Selling Like Hot cakes

 The plants, cakes and pickles sale was the next fund-raising event. The children had to plan ahead so that they had enough pot plants, jars of pickle and freshly baked cakes to sell on the day.

Home Cooking

There was lots of cooking to be done. The children got busy in the kitchen making the cakes and pickle.

Tasty treats

Little iced cakes, jam tarts and chocolate crispies sold for a few pence, but the money mounted up as everyone came back for more . . . and more . . . and more.

On the day of the sale there were plenty of goodies for everyone.

Green fingers

Preparations for the plant sale had to start early. In the spring, the children took cuttings from geraniums and sowed flower and vegetable seeds. When the seedlings had grown big enough, they were transplanted into pots ready for the summer plant sale.

I'll roll the pastry, you cut the cases, and you can do the jam.

These jam tarts smell delicious!

Watch us, and next time you can make the chocolate crispies.

Peeling and chopping all the vegetables for the pickle is hard work.

Adding Up

All their hard work made another £24.40 to add to the fund.

Sponsored Spell

A sponsor is someone who promises to give money to *charity* for something you achieve. For the next fund-raising event, the children had to find people willing to sponsor them for a sponsored spell.

These are the words the children had to spell.

Branscombe School Sponsored Spell

Younger children	Older children
going	bought
went	graph
where	mask
her	behaviour
come	soldier
riding	computer
school	member
little	remember
because	surface
fish	ground

The children enjoy their annual charity walk.

Sponsorship

The school already did a sponsored walk for charity every year, where a sponsor gives a walker a certain amount of money for every mile they walk. The children know that the more miles they walk and the more sponsors they find, the more money they will raise.

The sponsored spell

For the sponsored spell, the children had to go home and learn how to spell the ten words on their list. When they came back into school, they had to write them down to show that they knew them.

Michael worked hard to learn all his spellings.

Michael found the most sponsors and raised the most money.

> My grandma said, 'Let's go around the village.' Then I filled my form in and I tried to see if I could get any more people. We had to draw another bit of the form to fit them all on!

Adding up

The children raised another £210.40 from the sponsored spell to add to the fund.

Michael's form

Name	Amount per word	Number of words	Total due
Grandpa	30p	10 words	£3.00
Grandma	30p	10 words	£3.00

Finding sponsors

The children already knew how to find sponsors and fill in their forms because of the sponsored walk. Michael's parents, grandparents and great-grandparents have all lived in Branscombe, and several members of his family went to Branscombe School. Knowing a lot of people was very useful when it came to finding sponsors!

Lucky Dip and Penny Pots

The last fund-raising event was a lucky dip. The children decorated a large tub and eveyone donated prizes to go in it.

You have to wrap all the prizes in the same paper so that no one can guess what they are.

Pot luck

It's pot luck with a lucky dip - you pay your money and take a chance! You might get something you really want or something you don't want at all. You won't know until you tear off the paper.

Lucky dip

The lucky dip raised £25.20. At 20 pence a dip and with only 60 children in the school, everyone must have had at least two dips each! Perhaps the teachers were allowed to have a go too?

Penny pots

All the fund-raising ideas so far had been 'one-off' events. The penny pots were a 'long-term' fund-raising idea. They could make money for the community fund day after day.

 One penny pot sits on the counter at the Post Office.

Post office pot

The children asked if they could put one of their penny pots in the Post Office.
The answer was, 'Yes, of course!' Most of the Post Office customers know about the school's community fund and are happy to drop in a few pennies.

Questions

Can you think of another 'long-term' way of raising money?

Why can long-term money-raising be a good idea?

 Adding up

Every few weeks the children go down to the Post Office to check on their penny pot. So far, it has raised more than £100.

India Day

 Many special community events are organised by the school every year. One of the most popular was India Day. The children and some of their friends from nearby Farway school wanted to learn about life in an Indian community.

The whole community uses the village hall for meetings, plays, wedding receptions, dances and all kinds of other events. →

The village hall

The school building is very small, so when it's time for a party, a show or a special occasion, the whole school goes down the road to the village hall. This is where India Day took place.

Indian food

The children prepared Indian food at school and served it in the village hall. Some walkers who were passing by heard voices, smelled the delicious food and popped in for a free meal.

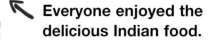 **Everyone enjoyed the delicious Indian food.**

Music and dancing

The children dressed in Indian clothes, watched a Hindu dancer and then learned the dance themselves. They played traditional musical instruments and learnt a Divali song

The children looked very bright and colourful in their Indian clothes. ↗

The lunch was outstandingly good. There were spicy potatoes, chicken curry and lots more.

There were lots of compliments for the children's food.

CHICKEN AND TURKEY CURRY

This is the recipe for the children's chicken and turkey curry. They needed lots of all the ingredients to feed so many people. If you want to try cooking this curry, make sure you ask an adult to help you.

Ingredients

Chicken   Turkey   Carrot   Onion   Spices
Water   Stock   Lemon juice

Recipe

1. Cut the chicken and turkey into bite-size pieces.
2. Slice the carrot and onion.
3. Roughly mix the spices together.
4. Add lemon juice and water to the spice mix.
5. Mix together the pieces of chicken, the sliced vegetables and the spices.
6. Heat the vegetable oil in a pan and fry the meat, vegetables and spices lightly.
7. Put everything in a big pot. Add the stock and water, and simmer gently until everything is tender.

The Harvest Lunch

 September is the traditional time to celebrate bringing in the harvest. Last year the school decided to hold a *Harvest Lunch*, and invited all the senior citizens of Branscombe.

The children sent out colourful invitations.

MENU

Harvest soup
Bread rolls
Apple
crumble
Custard

Harvest food

Then the Harvest Lunch menu was planned. As they were going to cook the food themselves, the children wanted to be sure it would be easy to cook and delicious. They decided on soup with bread rolls, followed by apple crumble and custard.

Invitations

The children wrote out Harvest Lunch invitations, posted them and received 100 acceptances! So many guests would never fit into the school. They would have to book the village hall again.

We sent invitations to lots of people in the village, and nearly all of them said they would come.

Making friends

On the day of the Harvest Lunch, the food was served by teachers and parents so that the children could sit with their guests. They all chatted and ate and made new friends.

The older people and the children found lots to talk about.

> It's given me lots of respect for the older people. I used to ride my skateboard really, really quickly and make lots of noise. Now I do blades instead because it's not so noisy.

Thank you!

The thank-you letters showed how much the guests had enjoyed themselves. One letter was special. It was from Mr Clarke, who wrote a thank-you poem called 'Harvest Lunch'. The poem was framed and hung up in the school for everyone to read.

"HARVEST LUNCH"

The children of Branscombe School, are such a Lovely Bunch
with Teachers and some Parents, they invited us to Lunch

Tables were laid around the Hall, with not an inch to spare
the children sat with the old folk, to show they really care

Then came a plate of nice hot soup, with bread roll and butter
and once we started eating, not one word did they mutter

It was the mums who broke the silence, from outside the kitchen door
with "Did you all enjoy that" and would you like some more

Soon the soup was over, but they were not finished yet
apple crumble and custard followed, the lovely taste we won't forget

The children were served cold drinks, and we had cups of tea
then entertainment was laid on, and all of this was free

Everyone was so well behaved, their teachers must be proud
and the talent of the performers, to play to such a crowd

On behalf of all who attended, For such a lovely day
God Bless the children and the teachers, plus Branscombe P.T.A.

C.W.E.Clarke
(Nobby)

The Millennium Orchard

The school's community project for the Year 2000 was to re-plant an apple orchard on the site of an old orchard in the village. It was a very big task and they would need some help. They knew who to ask – 🌿 THE NATIONAL TRUST

↑ The National Trust is a charity which protects buildings, the coast and the countryside so that people can enjoy them.

Working with the National Trust has helped the children respect wildlife and their environment. ↑

Working partners

Every year the National Trust works with the school on an **environmental** project. One year they helped the children to make bird boxes, and hung them from the trees in the woods behind the school to encourage birds to nest there.

Traditional trees

The plan was to plant traditional apple trees. The village would be able to enjoy their blossom in the spring and the apples in late summer. Twenty-two different varieties of apple were chosen. Some of them have very strange names: Star of Devon, Pig's Nose, Nine Square, Northcots Superb.

Adopt a tree

Before the planting started, everyone was asked if they wanted to adopt a tree and pay for its care. Some families asked for their tree to be dedicated to them. Other trees were dedicated to someone who had died. A Book of Dedication is kept at the school.

Here are some of the dedications for the trees

"My tree is planted in memory of the three most wonderful men in my life – my father, my uncle and my husband."

"This is a place that four generations of our family have loved and will continue to do so."

"In memory of my brother Brian (died aged 15), and a dedication to my daughters Olivia, Vikki, Elli and Abigail."

The Orchard Story

Planting took place on a cold, bright winter's day. Workers from the National Trust were already busy when the first group of children arrived. The young trees had been delivered and all the equipment was ready.

Digging holes was hard work. No one had dug the field for years and years.

Planting

Parents and grandparents, little brothers and sisters and school governors and friends, joined the children and helped them to dig and plant. Everyone who had bought a tree could choose where they would like to plant it.

Apple harvest

When the trees eventually grow big enough to produce apples, these apples can then be picked, free of charge, for two days during harvest time.

The delicate saplings were carefully planted and the earth around them trodden in. ↗

A fence was put up around each sapling to protect it. ↓

The villagers say thank you to Branscombe School.

> We are very grateful to the staff and children of Branscombe Primary School for their vision and dedication. This is one of the many projects that will really make a difference to the future life of this community.

Question

Why do you think an orchard is a good community project?

Glossary

Building Society
At a building society people can save money in a savings account or they can borrow money to buy a home.

Charity
A charity is an organisation that raises money and works for people who need help. Sometimes charities care for the environment or buildings.

Community
The community is the people who live together in a neighbourhood.

Disaster appeal
A disaster appeal is an appeal for money to provide immediate help when a disaster such as an earthquake, a flood or a famine takes place.

Environment
Your environment is everything that is around you, whether it is the countryside or a village, town or city.

Fund-raising
Fund-raising is raising money for a particular cause. Events such as a sponsored walk or a bring-and-buy sale raise money for the fund.

Harvest lunch
A harvest lunch or supper is held at harvest time when farmers bring in the crops such as wheat and corn. It is a celebration of a good harvest.

Interest
Interest is the money that is added to your savings in a building society. The more money in your savings account and the longer it stays there, the more interest it will earn.

Millennium
A millennium is a thousand years. The year 2000 marked the end of one millennium and the beginning of a new one.

Neighbourhood
Your neighbourhood is the place where you live. Your neighbours live near you in your neighbourhood.

Sponsor
To sponsor something is to support it with money. For a sponsored walk a sponsor will give a certain amount for every mile walked, or for a sponsored spell they will give money for every word spelled correctly.

Taking Part

Get involved

Branscombe School gets involved in the community and the community gets involved with the school.

Invite people from your community to come in and talk to you. Find out how they can help you and how you can help them.

Work with partners

Branscombe School works with the National Trust and the Alliance and Leicester Building Society on their community projects.

Find out which businesses and organisations – local, national or international – will work with you as partners on your projects.

Raise money

Schools often raise money for their own school funds. Branscombe School's community fund raises money to help other people.

You could work with a charity or take part in a national event such as Red Nose Day – then have fun raising money.

Plan a community project

Branscombe School plans a community project every year such as the Millennium Orchard and the Harvest Lunch for senior citizens.

You might be able to create or improve a facility that will benefit your whole community. You could plan an event, invite local people, get to know them and have a good time together.

Index